li

n

Jean Aitchison

(flash.

Hodder Education

338 Euston Road, London NW1 3BH.

Hodder Education is an Hachette UK company

First published in UK 2012 by Hodder Education.

Copyright © 2012 Jean Aitchison

The moral rights of the author have been asserted.

Database right Hodder Education (makers)

British Library Cataloguing in Publication Data: a catalogue record for this title is available from the British Library.

10 9 8 7 6 5 4 3 2 1

The publisher has used its best endeavours to ensure that any website addresses referred to in this book are correct and active at the time of going to press. However, the publisher and the author have no responsibility for the websites and can make no guarantee that a site will remain live or that the content will remain relevant, decent or appropriate.

The publisher has made every effort to mark as such all words which it believes to be trademarks. The publisher should also like to make it clear that the presence of a word in the book, whether marked or unmarked, in no way affects its legal status as a trademark.

Every reasonable effort has been made by the publisher to trace the copyright holders of material in this book. Any errors or omissions should be notified in writing to the publisher, who will endeavour to rectify the situation for any reprints and future editions.

Hachette UK's policy is to use papers that are natural, renewable and recyclable products and made from wood grown in sustainable forests. The logging and manufacturing processes are expected to conform to the environmental regulations of the country of origin.

www.hoddereducation.co.uk

Typeset by Cenveo Publisher Services.

Printed and bound by CPI Group (UK) Ltd., Croydon, CR0 4YY.

Also available
in ebook

Contents

1

what is linguistics?

This chapter explains what linguistics involves, and why it is important. It outlines the main subdivisions of the subject, and explains how linguistics differs from traditional grammar studies.

The use of language is an integral part of being human. Children all over the world start putting words together at approximately the same age, and follow remarkably similar paths in their speech development. All languages are surprisingly similar in their basic structure, whether they are found in South America, Australia or near the North Pole.

Linguistics tries to answer the basic questions 'What is language?' and 'How does language work?' It probes into various aspects of these problems, such as 'What do all languages have in common?', 'What range of variation is found among languages?', 'How does human language differ from animal communication?', 'How does a child learn to speak?', and so on.

What is a linguist?

A person who studies linguistics is usually referred to as a **linguist**. The word 'linguist' is unsatisfactory: it causes confusion, since it also refers to someone who speaks a large number of languages. Linguists in the sense of linguistics experts need not be fluent in languages, though they must have a wide experience of different types of language. It is more important for them to analyse and explain linguistic phenomena such as the Turkish vowel system, or German verbs, than to make themselves understood in Istanbul or Berlin.

How does linguistics differ from traditional grammar?

One frequently meets people who think that linguistics is old school grammar jazzed up with a few new names. But it differs in several basic ways.

First, and most important, linguistics is **descriptive**, not prescriptive. Linguists are interested in what *is* said, not what they think *ought* to be said. They describe language in all its aspects, but do not prescribe rules of 'correctness'.

The notion of absolute and unchanging 'correctness' is quite foreign to linguists. They might recognize that one type of speech appears, through the whim of fashion, to be more socially acceptable than others. But this does not make the socially acceptable variety any more interesting for them than the other varieties, or the old words any better than new ones. To linguists the language of a pop singer is not intrinsically worse (or better) than that of a duke.

A second important way in which linguistics differs from traditional school grammar is that linguists regard the spoken language as primary, rather than the written.

It preceded the written everywhere in the world, as far as we know. Moreover, most writing systems are derived from the vocal sounds. Although spoken utterances and written sentences share many common features, they also exhibit considerable differences. Linguists therefore regard spoken and written forms as belonging to different, though overlapping, systems, which must be analysed separately: the spoken first, then the written.

A third way in which linguistics differs from traditional grammar studies is that it does not force languages into a Latin-based framework. Many people have wrongly come to regard certain Latin categories as being 'natural' ones. For example, it is commonly assumed that the Latin tense divisions of past, present and future are inevitable. Yet one frequently meets languages which do not make this neat threefold distinction. In some languages, it is more important to express the duration of an action – whether it is a single act or a continuing process – than to locate the action in time.

In brief, linguists are opposed to the notion that any one language can provide an adequate framework for all the others. They are trying to set up a universal framework. And there is no reason why this should resemble the grammar of Latin, or the grammar of any other language arbitrarily selected from the thousands spoken by humans.

The scope of linguistics

Linguistics covers a wide range of topics and its boundaries are difficult to define.

A diagram in the shape of a wheel gives a rough impression of the range covered.

In the centre is **phonetics**, the study of human speech sounds. A good knowledge of phonetics is useful for a linguist. Yet it is a basic background knowledge, rather than part of linguistics itself. Phoneticians are concerned with the actual physical sounds, the raw material out of which language is made. Linguists, on the other hand, are more interested in the way in which language is patterned. They analyse the shape or **form** of these patterns rather than the physical substance out of which the units of language are made.

In Figure 1.1, phonetics is surrounded by **phonology** (sound patterning), then phonology is surrounded by **syntax**. The term 'syntax', used in its broadest sense, refers to both the

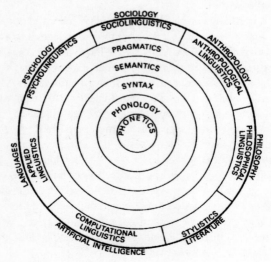

Figure 1.1.

GRAMMAR

| PHONOLOGY | SYNTAX | SEMANTICS |

Figure 1.2.

arrangement and the form of words. It is that part of language which links together the sound patterns and the meaning. **Semantics** (meaning) is placed outside syntax. Phonology, syntax and semantics are the 'bread and butter' of linguistics, and are a central concern of this book. Together they constitute the **grammar** of a language.

Around the central grammatical hub comes **pragmatics**, which deals with how speakers use language in ways which cannot be predicted from linguistic knowledge alone. This fast-expanding topic has connections both with semantics, and with the various branches of linguistics which link language with the external world.

These various branches overlap to some extent, so are hard to define clearly. Psycholinguistics, sociolinguistics and stylistics are perhaps the ones which have expanded fastest in recent years.

Finally, there are two important aspects of linguistics which have been omitted from the diagram. The first is **historical linguistics**, the study of language change. This omission was inevitable in a two-dimensional diagram. But if the wheel diagram is regarded as three-dimensional, as if it were the cross-section of a tree, then this topic can be included. A grammar can be described at one particular point in time (a single cut across the tree), or its development can be studied over a number of years, by comparing a number of different cuts made across the tree-trunk at different places.

The second omission is **linguistic typology**, the study of different language types. This could not be fitted in because it spreads over several layers of the diagram, covering phonology, syntax and semantics.

2

what is language?

This chapter outlines some important 'design features' of human language, and explores the extent to which they are found in animal communication. It also looks at the role of language in human life.

Linguistics can be defined as 'the systematic study of language' – a discipline which describes language in all its aspects and formulates theories as to how it works.

But what exactly *is* language? People often use the word in a very wide sense: 'the language of flowers', 'the language of music', 'body language' and so on. This book, in common with most linguistics books, uses the word to mean the specialized sound-signalling system which seems to be genetically programmed to develop in humans.

But can language be defined? And how can it be distinguished from other systems of animal communication? A useful approach is to make a list of **design features**, and to consider whether they are shared by other animals.

Use of sound signals

When animals communicate with one another, they may do so by a variety of means. Crabs, for example, communicate by waving their claws at one another, and bees have a complicated series of 'dances' which signify the whereabouts of a source of nectar.

But such methods are not as widespread as the use of sounds, which are employed by humans, grasshoppers, birds, dolphins, cows, monkeys, and many other species. So our use of sound is in no way unique.

Arbitrariness

There is often a recognizable link between the actual signal and the message an animal wishes to convey. An animal who wishes to warn off an opponent may simulate an attacking attitude. A cat, for example, will arch its back, spit and appear ready to pounce.

In human language, the reverse is true. In the great majority of cases, there is no link whatsoever between the signal and the message. The symbols used are **arbitrary**. There is no intrinsic connection, for example, between the word *elephant* and the animal it symbolizes. Nor is the phrase 'These bananas are bad' intrinsically connected with food. Onomatopoeic words such as *quack-quack* and *bang* are exceptions – but there are relatively few of these compared with the total number of words.

The need for learning

Many animals automatically know how to communicate without learning. Their systems of communication are genetically inbuilt. Bee-dancing, for example, is substantially the same in bee colonies in different parts of the world, with only small variations.

This is quite different from the long learning process needed to acquire human language, which is culturally transmitted. A human brought up in isolation simply does not acquire language, as is shown by the rare studies of children brought up by animals without human contact.

Duality

Animals which use vocal signals have a stock of basic sounds which vary according to species. A cow has under 10, a chicken has around 20, and a fox over 30. Dolphins have between 20 and 30, and so do gorillas and chimpanzees. Most animals can use each basic sound only once. That is, the number of messages an animal can send is restricted to the number of basic sounds, or occasionally the basic sounds plus a few simple combinations.

Human language works rather differently. Each language has a stock of sound units or **phonemes** which are similar in number to the basic sounds possessed by animals; the average number is between 30 and 40. But each phoneme is normally meaningless in isolation. It becomes meaningful only when it is combined with other phonemes. That is, sounds such as *f, g, d, o*, mean nothing separately. They normally take on meaning only when they are combined together in various ways, as in *fog, dog, god*.

This organization of language into two layers – a layer of sounds which combine into a second layer of larger units – is known as **duality** or **double articulation**. A communication system with duality is considerably more flexible than one without it, because a far greater number of messages can be sent.

Displacement

Most animals can communicate about things in the immediate environment only. A bird utters its danger cry only when danger is present. It cannot give information about a peril which is removed in time and place. This type of spontaneous utterance is nearer to a human baby's emotional cries of pain, hunger or contentment than it is to fully developed language.

Human language, by contrast, can communicate about things that are absent as easily as about things that are present. This apparently rare phenomenon, known as **displacement**, does occasionally occur in the animal world, for example, in the communication of honey bees. But even bees are limited in this ability. They can inform each other only about nectar. Human language can cope with any subject whatever, and it does not matter how far away the topic of conversation is in time and space.

Creativity (productivity)

Most animals have a very limited number of messages they can send or receive. The male of a certain species of grasshopper, for example, has a choice of six.

Not only is the number of messages fixed for the grasshopper, but so are the circumstances under which each can be communicated. All animals, as far as we know, are limited in a similar way. Bees can communicate only about nectar. Dolphins, in spite of their intelligence and large number of clicks, whistles and squawks, seem to be restricted to communicating about the same things again and again.

This type of restriction is not found in human language, which is essentially **creative** (or **productive**). Humans can produce novel utterances whenever they want to. A person can utter a sentence which has never been said before, in the most unlikely circumstances, and still be understood. If, at a party, someone said, 'There is a purple platypus crawling across the ceiling,' friends might think the speaker was drunk or drugged, but they would still understand the words spoken.

Patterning

Many animal communication systems consist of a simple list of elements. There is no internal organization within the system.

Human language, on the other hand, is most definitely not a haphazard heap of individual items. Humans do not juxtapose sounds and words in a random way. Instead, they ring the changes on a few well-defined patterns.

Take the sounds *a*, *b*, *s*, *t*. In English, there are only four possible ways in which these sounds could be arranged, *bats*, *tabs*, *stab* or *bast* 'inner bark of lime'. All other possibilities, such as * *sbat*, * *abts*, * *stba*, are excluded (an asterisk indicates an impossible word or sentence). The starred words are not excluded because such sequences are unpronounceable, but because the 'rules' subconsciously followed by people who know English do not allow these combinations, even for new words. A new washing powder called *Sbat* would be unlikely to catch on, since English does not permit the initial sequence *sb*, even though in some other languages (for example, ancient Greek) this combination is not unusual.

Similarly, consider the words *burglar*, *loudly*, *sneezed*, *the*. Here again, only three combinations are possible: *The burglar sneezed loudly*, *Loudly sneezed the burglar* and (perhaps) *The burglar loudly sneezed*. All others are impossible, such as * *The loudly burglar sneezed*, or * *Sneezed burglar loudly the*.

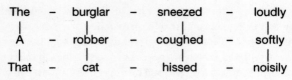

Figure 2.1.

Every item in language, then, has its own characteristic place in the total pattern. It can combine with certain specified items, and be replaced by others.

Language can therefore be regarded as an intricate network of interlinked elements in which every item is held in its place and given its identity by all the other items. No word (apart from the names of some people or objects) has an independent validity or existence outside that pattern. The elements of language can be likened to the players in a game of soccer. A striker, or a goal-keeper, has no use or value outside the game. But placed among the other players, a striker acquires an identity and value. In the same way, linguistic items such as *the*, *been*, *very*, only acquire significance as part of a total language network.

To summarize: language is a patterned system of arbitrary sound signals, characterized by creativity, displacement, duality and cultural transmission.

This is true of all languages in the world, which are remarkably similar in their main design features. There is no evidence that any language is more 'primitive' than any other. There are certainly primitive cultures. A primitive culture is reflected in the vocabulary of a language, which might lack words common in advanced societies. But even the most primitive tribes have languages whose underlying structure is every bit as complex as English or Russian or Chinese.

But one other similarity links human language with animal communication: it is predestined to emerge. Just as frogs inevitably croak, and cows moo, so humans are prearranged for talking.

Human infants are not born speaking, but they know how to acquire any language to which they are exposed. They are drawn towards the noises coming out of human mouths, and they instinctively know how to analyse speech sounds.

Origin of language

Language probably developed in east Africa, around 100,000 years ago.

But *why* did language begin? Social chit-chat, the meaningless small talk of everyday life, may have played a key role, as it does today: 'Hallo, how nice to see you. How are you? Isn't the weather terrible?'

The use of language for persuading and influencing others has probably always been important. Yet 'information talking' – swapping news and conveying essential commands – may not be as basic as was once assumed. It is prominent primarily in public forms of language, less so in private conversations, which form the bulk of day-to-day interactions.

Language can of course be used to communicate feelings and emotions, though this aspect of language is not well developed. Humans, like other primates, can convey emotions via screams, grunts, sobs, gestures and so on. So they need language only to confirm and elaborate these more primitive signals.

3

the study of language

This chapter sketches the main directions
linguistics has taken in the past two
centuries, and also makes some predictions
about future trends.

The discipline of linguistics can be likened to a pathway which is being cut through the dark and mysterious forest of language. Different parts of the forest have been explored at different times, so we can depict the path as a winding one.

As Figure 3.1 shows, there have been three major directions in linguistics in the past two centuries.

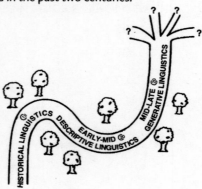

Figure 3.1.

Nineteenth century: historical linguistics

Before the nineteenth century, language in the Western world was of interest mainly to philosophers.

1786 is the year which many people regard as the birthdate of linguistics. In that year, an Englishman, Sir William Jones, pointed out that Sanskrit (the old Indian language), Greek, Latin, Celtic and Germanic all had striking structural similarities. So impressive were these likenesses that these languages must spring from one common source, he concluded.

Sir William Jones' discovery fired the imagination of scholars. For the next hundred years, other linguistic work was eclipsed by the general preoccupation with writing comparative grammars — grammars which first compared the different linguistic forms found in the various members of the Indo-European language family, and

INDO-EUROPEAN

| Indo-Iranian (Sanskrit, etc.) | Albanian | Armenian | Balto-Slavonic (Russian, etc.) | Greek | Italic (Latin, etc.) | Celtic (Welsh, etc.) | Germanic (German, English, etc.) |

Figure 3.2.

second, attempted to set up a hypothetical ancestor, Proto-Indo-European, from which all these languages were descended.

Early to mid-twentieth century: descriptive linguistics

In the twentieth century, the emphasis shifted from language change to language description. Instead of looking at how a selection of items changed in a number of different languages, linguists began to concentrate on describing single languages at one particular point in time.

In the USA, linguistics began as an offshoot of anthropology. Around the beginning of the twentieth century, anthropologists were eager to record the culture of the fast-dying American-Indian tribes, and the American-Indian languages were one aspect of this.

During this time, large numbers of linguists concentrated on writing descriptive grammars of unwritten languages. This involved first finding native speakers of the language concerned and collecting sets of utterances from them. Second, it involved analysing the corpus of collected utterances by studying the phonological and syntactic patterns of the language concerned.

Mid- to late twentieth century: generative linguistics and the search for universals

In 1957, linguistics took a new turning. Noam Chomsky, then aged 29, published a book called *Syntactic Structures*. Although containing fewer than 120 pages, this little book started a revolution in linguistics. Chomsky is, arguably, the most influential linguist of the twentieth century. Certainly, he is the linguist whose reputation has spread furthest outside linguistics. He has, in the opinion of many, transformed linguistics from a relatively obscure discipline of interest mainly to graduate students and future missionaries into a major social science of direct relevance not only to linguists, but also to psychologists, sociologists, anthropologists, philosophers and others.

Chomsky shifted attention away from detailed descriptions of actual utterances, and started asking questions about the nature of the system which produces the output.

Chomsky pointed out that anyone who knows a language must have internalized a set of rules which specify the sequences permitted in their language. In his opinion, a linguist's task was to discover these rules, which constitute the grammar of the language in question. Chomsky therefore used the word 'grammar' interchangeably to mean, on the one hand, a person's internalized rules, and on the other hand, a linguist's guess as to these rules. This is perhaps confusing, as the actual rules in a person's mind are unlikely to be the same as a linguist's hypothesis, even though there will probably be some overlap.

A grammar consisting of a set of statements or rules that specify which sequences of a language are possible, and which impossible, is a generative grammar.

Chomsky, therefore, initiated the era of generative linguistics. In his words, a grammar will be 'a device which generates all the grammatical sequences of a language and none of the ungrammatical ones'.

As well as initiating the era of generative grammars, Chomsky also redirected attention towards **language universals**. He pointed out that as all humans are rather similar, their internalized language mechanisms are likely to have important common properties. He argued that linguists should concentrate on finding elements and constructions that are *available* to all languages, whether or not they actually occur.

Above all, they should seek to specify the universal bounds or **constraints** within which human language operates.

The constraints on human language are, he suggested, inherited ones. Human beings may be preprogrammed with a basic knowledge of what languages are like, and how they work.

Twenty-first century: future trends

Chomsky's influence is a permanent one. An explosion of interest in language among non-linguists has been a valuable by-product of his work. He has directed attention towards the language potential of human beings, rather than the detailed description of linguistic minutiae. As a result, huge numbers of psychologists, neurologists, anthropologists, sociologists and philosophers have begun to take a greater interest in language and linguistics. Collaboration with them has led to the spiralling development of what were once 'fringe areas', such as psycholinguistics and sociolinguistics, but are now major – and still expanding – fields in their own right.

Of course, languages mostly do not vary wildly – they cluster around statistical norms. Linguistic statisticians, and also typologists, are beginning to estimate the degree to which a construction is 'natural' both within individual languages, and within human language as a whole. Hopefully, in the next century, we will have a much firmer grasp of linguistic 'norms', and how far they can be stretched. This hunt is now aided by **corpus linguistics**, the study and use of computerized databases for linguistic research.

4

deciding where to begin

This chapter points out that language can be explored in different ways, and outlines how this exploration can be carried out.

Language is an enormous and very complex phenomenon. If one wants to study it, where should one begin? People tend to argue about this. One way of studying something complex is to suggest that it is like something we humans already know something about.

Language as a game

Language can be regarded as a complicated type of game, assuming a 'game' to be 'a specified type of activity governed by rules'. The various facets involved in a game can show why there is some disagreement when linguists try to decide where to begin studying language.

In a typical game, such as chess or soccer, anyone trying to find out how the game is played has to deal with three broad types of question: the *aims of the game*, the *principles of interaction*, and the *permitted moves*.

Under the **aims of the game**, comes the fundamental question: what are people trying to do when they play it? In soccer, the players are trying to kick the ball into a net in order to score. The 'aims' of language involve not only the broad functions (conveying information, expressing emotion, keeping in touch socially, and so on), but also more specific purposes for which language can be used, such as:

Obtain information: *Where's the parrot?*
Make someone do something: *Shut the door!*
Make a promise: *I'll pay you next week.*

The **principles of interaction** involve questions such as: How many people can play? Do they all play at the same time, or do they take it in turns? If so, how does one know when a person's turn is over? Within language, people take it in turns to speak, and each language tends to have certain socially prescribed 'turns'. For example, in English, a greeting is usually followed by another greeting:

John: *Good morning, Felicity.*
Felicity: *Why hallo there, John.*

Under **permitted moves,** linguists explore which 'moves' are permitted, and which not. In chess, some pieces can move across the board only in straight lines, and others only diagonally. With regard to language, there are rules underlying well-formed sequences of a language. In English, for example, verbs precede their objects, as in *The cat ate the canary*, rather than * *The cat the canary ate* which would be the standard order in, say, Turkish.

When dealing with language, one might at first sight want to tackle these facets in the order listed above. But in practice, there is a problem. It is easier to specify the basic permitted moves than it is to give a clear account of the aims and principles of interaction, which are closely interwoven with the social structures of the society involved. For this reason, the majority of professional linguists prefer to begin with those aspects of language which can most easily be detached from the social background. They therefore start with the permitted moves or, in linguistic terminology, the grammar of the language. They consider this to be the core of linguistic study, and expect to add on its interrelationships with society at a later stage.

In this book, therefore, we shall be moving from the basic linguistic core outwards. In other words, we shall start from the centre of the circle diagram shown in Chapter 1 (Figure 1.1), and move out to the edges later. But a decision as to where to begin does not necessarily imply an overall order of importance: people put on their socks before their shoes, but they are not necessarily giving more importance to socks than to shoes.

5

sound patterns

This chapter explains how linguists represent the flow of speech, and outlines the type of symbols used. It also discusses sound combinations, and points out that some languages distinguish words via differences in pitch (tone languages).

Linguistics is concerned primarily with the spoken word. So a priority task for anyone describing sounds is to decide how to represent the flow of speech. Clearly, the conventional written forms are most unsatisfactory, since they often provide little guide to pronunciation.

Linguists, then, when they are concerned with sounds, abandon conventional spelling for the purpose of representing spoken utterances, and use one of the many specially devised systems of notation in which one symbol represents one sound. Perhaps the best known of these is the International Phonetic Alphabet (IPA). A number of IPA symbols are borrowed from the conventional written alphabet:

[b] as in '*b*ird'
[d] as in '*d*og'

(Symbols representing sounds are put into square brackets.)

Other symbols are variations of alphabet letters:

[ɒ] as in 'h*o*t' is an upside-down *a*.
[ŋ] as in 'ba*ng*' is a combination of *n* and *g*.
[ɪ] as in 'h*i*t' is a small-size capital I.

Sometimes obsolete letters are used:

[ʃ] as in di*sh*.

Other symbols are from the Greek alphabet:

[θ] as in *th*in,

and a few symbols are inventions:

[ɬ] Welsh *ll* as in *Ll*anelli.

Sometimes supplementary marks are added to the symbols. For example, two dots indicate length:

[uː] (long *u*) as in b*oo*t.

By such means, the IPA has built up a store of symbols which can, in theory, represent any sound in any language.

Sorting out the basic sounds

Let us assume that a linguist is working on a hitherto unknown, unwritten language. The first step is to find a suitable informant – a reliable native speaker from whom to gather samples of speech. The early sessions will concentrate on the accurate transcription of sounds, dealing at first with single words.

As time goes by, and as the sounds of the language under investigation become familiar, the linguist will transcribe more and more accurately. Simultaneously, it will slowly become apparent that the variety of strange sounds is not infinite. Instead, the informant is ringing the changes on a relatively small number of basic sounds or **phonemes**, each of which may have several variant forms.

The number of phonemes varies from language to language. The average is around 35. English has 44, according to a well-known analysis of one widely spoken variety of British English.

A **phoneme** is the smallest segment of sound which can distinguish two words. Take the words *pit* and *bit*. These differ only in their initial sound, *pit* begins with /p/ and *bit* begins with /b/. This is the smallest amount by which these two words could differ and still remain distinct forms. Any smaller subdivision would be impossible, because English does not subdivide /p/ or /b/.

In addition to identifying and analysing the phonemes of a language, a linguist must also work out ways in which the phonemes may be combined. Every language has certain permitted sequences of sounds, and others which are not allowed.

In English, for example, a word which begins with three consonant-type phonemes always obeys three strict rules:

1 *The first phoneme must be /s/.*
2 *The second phoneme must be /p/ or /t/ or /k/.*
3 *The third phoneme must be /l/ or /r/ or /w/ or /j/.*

The result is that all words beginning with three consonants are words such as *spring, string* or *splendid*. We never find words such as **bdling, *sgteal* or **wbtendid*.

6

words and pieces of words

This chapter looks at the problems encountered in identifying and defining the notion 'word'. It then briefly discusses 'morphemes' (meaningful chunks of words). Finally, it looks at how words can be assigned to 'word classes' (parts of speech).

The **word** appears to be a widespread concept. Even in primitive cultures, informants are often able to identify words. This is somewhat surprising, because nobody has yet proposed a satisfactory universal definition of the notion 'word', or provided a foolproof method of identification. People sometimes wrongly assume that a word is recognizable because it represents a 'single piece of meaning'. But it can easily be shown that this view is wrong by looking at the lack of correspondence between words from different languages. In English, the three words *cycle repair outfit* correspond to one in German, *Fahrradreparaturwerkzeuge*.

Why have linguists found it so hard to find a satisfactory definition of the notion 'word'? The answer seems to be that there are different types of word. Consider the rhyme:

> *A flea and a fly in a flue*
> *Were imprisoned, so what could they do?*
> *Said the flea: 'Let us fly'.*
> *Said the fly: 'Let us flee'.*
> *So they flew through a flaw in the flue.*

At the simplest level, this rhyme contains 36 written words. On closer examination, we come up against several problems. Should *fly* (noun) and *fly* (verb) be counted as the same, since they sound the same, or as different, because they have different meanings? Should *fly* and *flew* be regarded as the same, because they belong to the same verb, or as different because they have different forms? These problems can be solved only if we decide what kind of 'word' we are talking about.

If by 'word' we mean **lexical item** (the technical term for 'dictionary entry'), then the sound sequence /flaɪ/ 'fly' represents two words, since most dictionaries have separate entries for *fly* (noun, N) and *fly* (verb, V):

fly N: an insect with two wings.
fly V: to move through the air in a controlled manner.

This is perhaps the most basic, and most abstract use of the word 'word'. However, both of these lexical items have various syntactic forms associated with them. The insect could occur as *fly* (singular) or flies (plural), and the verb could occur as *fly*, *flying*, *flies*, *flew*, *flown*.

A further complication occurs with a lexical item such as *flaw*. This has the two syntactic forms *flaw* (singular) and *flaws* (plural). But the singular form *flaw* then has two different sound sequences associated with it, /flɔː/ before a consonant, and /flɔːr/ before a vowel:

> *The flue had a flaw /flɔː/ which allowed the fly to escape.*
> *There was a flaw /flɔːr/ in the flue.*

These examples show that we must not expect an exact overlap between different types of word. And in some other languages, the situation is far more complex than in English. In Latin, for example, the lexical item *rosa*, 'rose', has 12 different syntactic forms. In Welsh, the initial consonant of each word varies systematically, depending mainly on the preceding sound: the word for 'father' could be *tad*, *dad*, *thad*, or *nhad*.

Identifying words

For anyone working on an unknown language, it is important to identify these various types of word. There are two main stages in the analysis. First, finding chunks such as *fly*, *flew*, which recur as self-contained units. Second, deciding how many lexical items are covered by each chunk (as with *fly*, which covers two lexical items), and conversely, deciding how many different chunks belong to the same lexical item (as with *fly*, *flew*, where different syntactic forms belong to one lexical item).

For the first stage, finding chunks which behave as self-contained units, we look for sequences which are **uninterruptible** and **mobile**. These are useful guidelines in many languages. A sequence such as *chickens* cannot be interrupted. It is impossible to say * *chick-little-ens*, or * *chicken-little-s*. In addition, the sequence *chickens* can move about. It can occur next to different words, and in different parts of the sentence, as in: *Chickens lay eggs, foxes eat chickens, the chickens clucked loudly*, and so on.

At the end of this stage of the analysis, we have a rough list of 'words', though a list in which we are likely to have clumped together different lexical items which sound the same (**homonyms**), and to have separated different syntactic forms of the same lexical item.

For the second stage of the analysis, we need to consider the syntactic behaviour of these possible 'words', that is, their role in the overall sentence pattern. For example, *fly* N would show up as behaving differently from *fly* V, since each would fit into a different 'slot' in the sentences:

The fly *buzzed.*
Birds fly.

On the other hand, *fly* and *flew* would turn out to be somewhat similar, in that they would fit into the same general slot:

They fly home on Sunday.
They flew home on Sunday.

However, the syntactic behaviour of these different forms can be supplemented by an analysis of their make-up, or, in other words, the **morphemes** out of which they are constituted.

Morphemes

The smallest syntactic unit is the **morpheme**. Morphemes vary in size. Neither syllables nor length are any guide to their identification. The essential criterion is that a morpheme cannot be cut up into smaller syntactic segments.

The sentence in Figure 6.1 has eleven morphemes:

The	sleep	walk	ing	albatross	chant	ed	a	dream	y	lullaby
1	2	3	4	5	6	7	8	9	10	11

Figure 6.1.

The, albatross, a, lullaby, are all single morphemes because none of them can be syntactically split up further. *Alba-* and *-tross*, for example, do not have any other role to play in the syntax of English: they exist only as part of the single unit, *albatross. Chanted* and *dreamy*, on the other hand, each consist of two morphemes: *chant* is found in words such as *chanting, chants*, and is also a word by itself, while *-ed* is found in *wanted, batted* and so on. Similarly, *sleep-walking* consists of three morphemes, because *sleep, walk* and *-ing* are all found elsewhere. In theory there is no upper limit to the number of morphemes per word: *antidisestablishmentarianism*, for example, has at least six: *anti-dis-establish-ment-arian-ism.*

Recognition of morphemes

Linguists identify morphemes by comparing a wide variety of utterances. They look for utterances which are partially the same (Figure 6.2):

The	dinosaur	sniff-**ed**	arrogant-**ly**	and	plodd-**ed**	for-**wards**
The	dinosaur	grunt-**ed**	loud-**ly**	and	edg-**ed**	back-**wards**

Figure 6.2.

The partial similarity between *sniffed, grunted, plodded* and *edged* enables one to isolate the segment *-ed*. And the partial similarity between *arrogantly* and *loudly*, and between *backwards* and *forwards*, makes it possible to isolate *-ly* and *-wards*.

Not all morphemes are as easily segmentable as these examples. But the identification of morphemes is done wholly by means of this one basic technique – the comparison of partially similar utterances.

Types of morpheme

Consider the sentence:

The owl look-ed *up at the* cloud-y *sky.*

Superficially, both *looked* and *cloudy* have a similar make-up. Yet -*ed* on the end of *looked* is an **inflectional** morpheme, since it provides further information about an existing lexical item, *look*, in this case indicating that the looking occurred in the past. Other examples of inflectional morphemes are the plural, as in *owls*, and the possessive, as in *Peter's car*. However, -*y* on the end of *cloud*y behaves rather differently. It is a **derivational** morpheme, one which creates an entirely new word. *Cloud* and *cloudy* behave quite differently and fit into different slots in the sentence. Other examples of derivational morphemes are -*ness* as in *happiness*, -*ish* as in *greenish*, and -*ment* as in *establishment*.

In most cases, it is easy to tell the difference between inflection and derivation. Above all, inflectional endings do not alter the syntactic behaviour of an item in any major way. The word still fits into the same 'slot' in the sentence. Derivational endings create entirely new words. In addition, inflectional endings can be added on to derivational ones, but not vice-versa. That is, we find words such as *establish-ment-s*, but not **establish-s-ment*.

Word classes

In every language, there are a limited number of types of lexical item. These different kinds of word are traditionally known as 'parts of speech', though in linguistic terminology the label **word class** is more common. Word classes are conventionally given labels, such as noun, verb, adjective.

Words are classified into word classes partly on account of their syntactic behaviour, partly on the basis of their morphological form. That is, words from the same word class are likely to fit into the same slot in a sentence, and to be inflected in similar ways. For example, the word class traditionally known as 'verb' can be recognized as a verb partly because it occurs after nouns (or phrases containing a noun), and partly because most verbs have an inflectional ending -ed to indicate the past:

> *Arabella detested snails.*
> *Marianna smiled.*

It is not always easy to tell how many word classes a language contains. Many traditional textbooks claim that English has eight 'parts of speech'. But this claim turns out to be based largely on old Latin grammars which were in turn translated from ancient Greek grammars, which mostly divided Greek words into eight word classes. If we look more closely, we find several discrepancies. For example, nouns and pronouns are traditionally classified as separate parts of speech, yet they have a large number of similarities:

> *Max laughed.*
> *He laughed.*

In fact, nouns and pronouns are more alike than the different types of word which are traditionally labelled adverbs. Words such as *quickly* and *very* are both usually classified as adverbs, but they behave quite differently:

> *He ran quickly.*
> **He ran very.*

The number of word classes varies from language to language. Some word classes, such as noun and verb, may be universal. But others vary. Nouns, adjectives and verbs are on a continuum. At one end are nouns, words which maintain their identity over time, such as *tree, cat, river*. At the other end are verbs, words which signify rapid change, as in *walk, kick, push*. In the middle come properties, such as *large, beautiful, old*. In English, these form a separate word class, that of adjectives. But this is not inevitable. Some languages treat them as a type of verb. Where English says:

> *Petronella is happy*

a language such as Chinese might say, as it were:

> *Petronella happies*

using a verb instead of an adjective. English also sometimes flips between verbs and adjectives. Compare the archaic *he ails* (stative verb) with the modern day *he is ill* (adjective).

Major word classes

English is sometimes considered to have four major word classes: noun (N), adjective (A), verb (V), preposition (P) (Figure 6.3).

Big	frogs	swim	under	water
A	N	V	P	N

Figure 6.3.

Of these four major classes, nouns, verbs and prepositions behave fairly differently from one another, though adjectives are somewhat strange, in that they have some noun-like qualities, and some verb-like ones. In *Blessed are the **brave**, brave* seems to have become a noun. And in *Mavis is **asleep**, asleep* seems fairly verb-like, since it fits into the same slot as *sleeping* in a sentence such as *Mavis is sleeping*.

The major word classes are known as **lexical categories**. Lexical categories contain **content** words, those with intrinsic meaning. They contrast with **functional categories**, which include 'little words' whose meaning is often difficult to specify, such as *the*, *a*, which are **determiners (D)**, or the **complementizer** *that* in *I know that Paul is ill*, often abbreviated to **COMP** or **C**.

These function words are important for gluing pieces of sentences together into longer syntactic patterns. These longer patterns will be the topic of the next chapter.

7

sentence patterns

This chapter discusses the ways in which words can be linked together to form larger units. It explains how to analyze sentences into their 'constituents' (component parts), and shows how to represent this type of analysis.

Words by themselves, or words strung together in a random way, are of relatively little use, a fact known by anyone who has visited a foreign country armed only with a dictionary, and no knowledge of the language. Does *me – bus* mean 'I am a bus', 'A bus hit me', 'I came by bus', or 'I want to go by bus'? So let us now look at how words may be combined together into longer utterances.

Linking words together

Different languages use different devices for showing the relationship of one word to another. Most languages have one or two favourite devices. The following are especially common.

Word order

The device used most frequently in English is **word order**:

The large spider frightened Aunt Matilda.
Aunt Matilda frightened the large spider.

The words themselves in these two sentences are identical. It is the word order which indicates who frightened whom, and that it is the spider which is large, not Aunt Matilda.

Inflections

In a language such as Latin, word endings or **inflections** indicate the relationship between words. In the sentence:

Magna aranea perterruit Matildam amitam.
Large spider frightened Matilda aunt
'The large spider frightened Aunt Matilda'.

the word order is irrelevant. The sentence would still mean the same if the words were arranged quite differently.

The endings alone show that it was the spider which terrified Aunt Matilda, not the reverse, and that it is the spider, not Aunt Matilda, which is large.

Function words

Another common device, is the use of **function words**. These are words such as *of*, *by*, *that*, which indicate relationships between parts of the sentence:

> *Aunt Matilda was terrified* **by** *a spider.*
> *The Queen* **of** *Sheba.*
> *I know* **that** *Penelope will come.*

Constituent analysis

Sentences are not simply random words strung together by means of various devices. We do not find English sentences such as:

> **The large spider terrified Aunt Matilda swims of Sheba by a car.*

Instead, English (like every other language) has a limited number of recurring sentence patterns. A fundamental technique of syntactic analysis is to identify these patterns by a process of successive substitution. Take the sentence:

> *The duck bit the burglar.*

In this sentence, *the* and *duck* can be replaced by a single word such as *Donald*, or *it*, without altering the basic sentence pattern. This suggests that these two words are closely linked, and together constitute a single, larger component. Similarly, the words *the* and *burglar* go together, since they also could be replaced by a word such as *Albert*, or *him*. So as a first stage, we have reduced a sentence with five original components down to three more basic ones.

| The duck | bit | the burglar |

Figure 7.1.

Of these three components, the final two could be replaced by a single word such as *slept*. We therefore conclude that they could be bracketed together as a single, larger component. We have therefore reduced a sentence with five components down to a basic two:

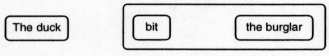

Figure 7.2.

The linguistic procedure which divides sentences into their component parts or constituents in this way is known as **constituent analysis**.

Tree diagrams

The successive layers of constituents which make up a sentence can be shown most clearly on a **tree diagram** – so called because its branches resemble the branches of an upside-down tree. In a tree diagram, a basic sentence type at the top branches downwards in ever-increasing complexity (Figure 7.3).

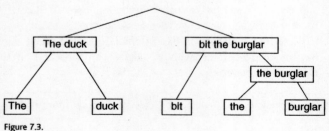

Figure 7.3.

The advantage of a tree diagram is that each join or **node** on the tree can be labelled, so that the whole construction becomes clearer (Figure 7.4).

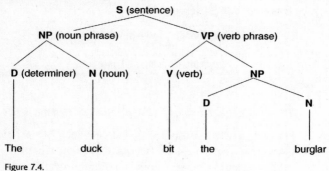

Figure 7.4.

Complex sentences

So far, we have assumed that all sentences are simple ones such as:

> *The duck bit the burglar.*
> *The mouse ran up the clock.*

In practice, however, many sentences have one or more sentence-like structures attached to them or inserted inside them. Consider:

> *Archibald played tennis, and Peter went fishing.*

Here we have two sub-sentences of equal importance attached together to form a single one. This process is known as **conjoining**. In theory an indefinite number of sentences could be joined together:

> *Archibald played tennis, and Peter went fishing, and Pip played cricket, and Mary washed her hair, and Drusilla climbed the Eiffel Tower...*

However, conjoining is not the only process by which sentence-like structures are linked together. More often subsidiary sentences are inserted into one main sentence. This is known as **embedding** (Figure 7.5):

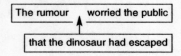

Figure 7.5.

The rumour that the dinosaur had escaped worried the public.

In theory, a sentence can have an indefinite number of sentences embedded in it. In *The fact that the rumour that the dinosaur had escaped worried the public is not surprising*, the simple sentence has two others embedded in it (Figure 7.6).

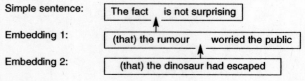

Figure 7.6.

Another example of embedding is the old nursery rhyme (Figure 7.7).

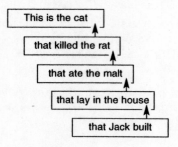

Figure 7.7.

Both embedding and conjoining illustrate an important property of language – that of **recursion**.

Recursion is the possibility of repeatedly reusing the same construction, so that there is no fixed limit to the length of sentences. This has important implications. It means that we can never make a complete list of all the possible sentences of any language. Instead, we must work out the system of rules which underlie the sentences.

meaning

This chapter explains what linguists are trying to do when they deal with 'semantics', the study of meaning. It shows how the meanings of 'lexical items' (words) are linked together in lexical structures. It shows that the study of synonyms (similar meaning words) and opposites can be useful. They provide valuable clues to the ways in which a language organizes its vocabulary.

The study of meaning is normally referred to as **semantics**. A linguist who is studying meaning tries to understand why certain words and constructions can be combined together in a semantically acceptable way, while others cannot. For example, it is quite all right to say:

My brother is a bachelor.
The camel sniffed the chocolate and then ate it.
The platypus remained alive for an hour after the hunter shot it.
Socrates arrived yesterday.

but not:

!My brother is a spinster.
!The camel swallowed the chocolate and then ate it.
!The platypus remained alive for an hour after the hunter killed it.
!Socrates arrived tomorrow.

These sentences are all well formed syntactically: nouns, verbs, and so on are all in the right order. But they are contradictory. An English hearer could interpret them only by assuming that the speaker has made a mistake, in which case they would say, for instance, 'A brother *can't* be a spinster, you must mean "bachelor" '. (An exclamation mark indicates a semantically impossible sentence.)

A linguist studying semantics would also like to know why anyone who knows a language can recognize certain phrases and sentences as having similar meanings, and would ask how it is that people can recognize:

Indicate to me the route to my habitual abode,
I am fatigued and I wish to retire,

as roughly equivalent to:

Show me the way to go home,
I'm tired and I want to go to bed,

A further human ability which needs explaining is the fact that hearers not only recognize ambiguous sentences, but they can also use the surrounding context to choose the most likely of the possible interpretations. For example:

Visiting great-aunts can be a nuisance.

is ambiguous. Are the great-aunts coming to see us, or are we going to see them? But if someone came across the sentence:

Visiting great-aunts can be a nuisance: I wish we didn't have to go.

they would have no doubt that we are visiting the great-aunts, rather than vice versa.

Word meaning

Clearly, the question of meaning is to a large extent connected with the meaning of individual words. So in a sentence such as:

!My brother is a spinster.

we need to find out about the meaning of *brother* and *spinster* in order to see why this sequence is unacceptable.

Meaning is double-faced. The meaning of a lexical item such as *tree* must be considered in two ways: first of all, as one element in a language system, whose 'meaning' is dependent on relationships with the other words in the system. Second, its 'meaning' is linked up with a certain class of recognizable objects in the external world (Figure 8.1).

Linguists regard these two aspects as complementary: they examine first one, then the other, starting with the **internal** relationships between linguistic elements.

LANGUAGE SYSTEM	OUTSIDE WORLD
bush | tree ← TREE → | wood etc.	

Figure 8.1.

As with all linguistic elements, every lexical item has its own particular place in the pattern. By studying the relationships of individual items, linguists can build up a picture of the overall structure of a language's vocabulary. When they do this they must forget that a word such as *apple* refers to an objectively identifiable object in the outside world, and must concentrate solely on its relationships with the other items in the language.

Semantic fields

Every language cuts up the world in different ways. It is not simply that one language sometimes has more subdivisions than another in certain areas. For example, Arabic has numerous words for different types of camel, where English has a variety of words for different types of dog. The situation is far more complicated. The set of words covering a certain area in one language is unlikely to correspond to those in any other language.

For example, it is impossible to translate the sentence *The cat sat on the mat* accurately into French without further information about the state of affairs described. We would have to decide arbitrarily whether the cat was sitting on a doormat (*paillasson*), a small rug (*tapis*), or a bedside mat (*descente de lit*). None of the French words corresponds exactly to our word 'mat' or 'rug' or 'carpet'.

These examples show us that for linguists, it is important to deal with the lexical structure of a language rather than with isolated words. The word *green* in English only becomes meaningful in relation to its neighbours in the set of colour terms: it denotes the colour between blue and yellow. Purple denotes the colour between red and blue. In semantics, as in phonology and syntax, language is not an accidental junk-heap consisting of a haphazard collection of different items. Instead, it is more like a jigsaw puzzle, where each piece fits into those which surround it, and where an isolated piece simply does not make sense if it is moved from its place in the overall pattern.

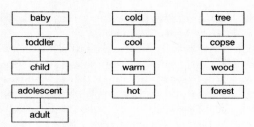

Figure 8.2.

In such a situation, it is useful to look at groups of lexical items which seem to belong together, sometimes known as a **lexical field**. Each item in a group or **set** can be defined by its place in relation to the other members of the set. *Adolescent* denotes someone who is no longer a child, but not yet an adult. *Cool* is the temperature between cold and warm. For many people, *copse* refers to an entity between a tree and a wood (Figure 8.2).

Such a study can give a useful picture of the way in which a particular semantic area is divided up. It would be wrong, however, to assume that lexical items cover an entire field like a smooth mosaic. In fact, there are plenty of gaps and overlaps. In English, a gap is sometimes claimed to exist in the field of dead objects. We have a word *corpse* meaning 'body of dead human being' and *carcase* meaning 'body of dead animal', but no comparable word for a dead plant.

Synonyms and opposites

To gain a fuller understanding of how lexical items hang together within a language, we need to look at the different types of relationship which exist between words. For example, the **synonyms** and **opposites** of a word can give valuable insights into its links with the rest of the vocabulary.

Lexical items can be regarded as synonymous if they can be interchanged without altering the meaning of an utterance:

He snapped the twig in half.
He broke the twig in half.

By studying interchangeable items, a linguist can build up a picture of those with similar meanings.

Perfect synonymy is rare. That is, it is very unusual for two lexical items to have exactly the same meanings in all contexts. Occasionally, such synonymy is found between formal and informal vocabulary items. For example, *rubella* is the term found in medical literature for the disease that is more generally known as *German measles*. But, usually, a lexical item only partially overlaps another, and the two are synonymous only in certain contexts.

To return to the words *snap* and *break*:

> *He snapped his fingers.*

does not mean the same as

> *He broke his fingers.*

And although

> *He broke the record for the 100-metre sprint.*

is an acceptable sentence,

> *He snapped the record for the 100-metre sprint.*

would seem unusual to most English speakers.

The study of opposites is more complex, as there are several different types of opposite.

The most obvious type is a pair of words in which the negative of one implies the other:

> *He is not married: he is single.*
> *He is not single: he is married.*

A second type of opposite is one which is not absolute, but relative to some standard. *Small* and *large*, for example, always imply some comparison:

> *What a large mouse!* (= what a large mouse in comparison to a normal-sized mouse)

What a small elephant! (= what a small elephant in comparison to a normal-sized elephant)

Classification (inclusion)

A further way of examining lexical structure is to note the ways in which a language classifies items. In English, for example, claret and hock are classified as 'wines'. Tea and coffee are referred to as 'beverages'. And wines and beverages both come under the heading of 'drinks'.

This indicates that the vocabulary of a language is partially hierarchically structured. In Figure 8.3 below, more general items come at the top, and more specific items are subdivisions of these:

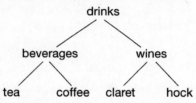

Figure 8.3.

Fuzziness and family resemblances

So far, we have assumed that words have an agreed-upon meaning which we can discover and describe. But this is true only of some lexical items. For others, it seems to be impossible to agree upon a 'proper meaning'.

In brief, with some words, there is a relatively high level of agreement as to which properties constitute an essential part of their meaning, but with others, no such agreement is found.

Fuzziness is another problem. Words often have fuzzy edges. There is no absolute divide between a cup and a mug, a glass and a vase, or a plate and a saucer. They all merge into one another. People use them inconsistently, calling something a *vase* one day, and a *glass* the next. They might call it a *vase* if it held flowers, and a *glass* if it held orange juice.

Family resemblances create further difficulties. Sometimes a word such as *furniture* covers a whole range of things, which share characteristics with one another, as do members of a family. Yet it may be impossible to think up a set of characteristics which describes them all.

These problems indicate that it is impossible to set down fixed meanings for all words. Humans, it turns out, understand one another not by learning fixed definitions, but by working from a **prototype**, or typical example. A prototypical bird is likely to be something like a robin, with a beak, wings, stick-like legs, and an ability to fly. A penguin or an emu is still sufficiently like a bird to be regarded as a bird, even though it is not such a 'normal' or prototypical bird. This flexibility allows a great number of things to be classified as birds, even a one-legged, one-winged parrot without a beak.

Making sense of the world

But what are these shadowy prototypes, and where do they come from? Humans, it appears, build themselves **mental models** in order to make sense of the world around them. In a simple case, as with birds, they decide which bird is the 'best' or most typical bird. But they also form ideas about more abstract concepts, often based on their own culture. English speakers regard a *week* as having seven days, divided into five working days followed by a weekend – though nothing in the external world forces this viewpoint. In other parts of the world, a week may have a different number of days. An Inca week had nine: eight working days, then market day on which the king changed his wives. Or take the word *mother*. Western parents assume that a *mother* is someone who not only gives birth to a child, but also usually looks after it and lives with the father – a culturally based picture, which is not necessarily true around the globe. Similarly, many people in England claim they live in a layered society, with upper-class, middle-class and working-class tiers, a notion inherited from books and newspapers. And so on, and so on.

The term **mental model** was coined by psychologists for the images people construct of the world. But the phenomenon is of wide interest, and other names have been adopted. The word **representation** is preferred by those working in cultural studies. This term covers not only subconscious or inherited representations, but also those consciously put across by, say, politicians, when they invent euphemisms such as *pin-point strikes* to lead people into believing that bombs can be precisely dropped on particular targets. The use of metaphor in both propaganda and poetry will be further discussed later in the book.

using language

This chapter discusses 'pragmatics', which explores aspects of meaning not predictable from the linguistic structure. It explores ways in which humans might do this, outlining the claim that humans cooperate with one another when they talk. It also discusses turn-talking and politeness in conversation.

'This is a self-clearing cafeteria' ran the notice in the student cafeteria. One might expect the plates and cups to put themselves away, judging from other similar phrases in the language, such as *self-cleaning oven*, *self-raising flour*, *self-righting lifeboat*. Yet the majority of students interpreted the phrase as meaning that they, the customers, were expected to clear away their plates. Why? The obvious answer is that they used their common sense and knowledge of the world to come to the most plausible interpretation in the circumstances, which was not necessarily the one most consistent with the linguistic structure.

Pragmatics is the branch of linguistics that studies those aspects of meaning which cannot be captured by semantic theory. In brief, it deals with how speakers use language in ways which cannot be predicted from linguistic knowledge alone. In a narrow sense, it deals with how listeners arrive at the intended meaning of speakers. In its broadest sense, it deals with the general principles followed by human beings when they communicate with one another.

The cooperative principle

An American philosopher, Paul Grice, is sometimes regarded as the 'father of pragmatics'. Grice emphasized that human beings communicate efficiently because they are by nature helpful to one another. He attempted to specify the principles which underlie this cooperative behaviour, and proposed four 'maxims' or rules of conversation.

1 *Maxim of quantity* Give the right amount of information when you talk. If someone at a party asked 'Who's that person with Bob?', a cooperative reply would be 'That's his new girlfriend, Alison.' An uncooperative reply would be an over-brief one, such as 'A girl', or an over-long one, such as 'That's Alison Margaret Jones, born 20 years ago in Kingston, Surrey, daughter of Peter and Mary Jones ... etc.'

2 *Maxim of quality* Be truthful. For example, if someone asked you the name of an unfamiliar animal, such as a platypus, reply truthfully, and don't say 'It's a kookaburra,' or 'It's a duck,' if you know it's a platypus.

3 *Maxim of relevance* Be relevant. If someone says, 'What's for supper?', give a reply which fits the question, such as 'Fish and chips', and not 'Tables and chairs' or 'Buttercups are yellow.'

4 *Maxim of manner* Be clear and orderly. For example, describe things in the order in which they occurred: 'The plane taxied down the runway, and took off to the west' rather than 'The plane took off to the west and taxied down the runway,' which might confuse people as to what actually happened.

At this outline level, the **cooperative principle** seems like common sense. It becomes more interesting when we consider how often people apparently break it. In answer to the question: 'What's for supper?' one is likely to receive a reply such as, 'Billy fell downstairs,' which doesn't answer the query. In answer to a question: 'Why don't you like Pamela?' one might get the response: 'Pamela's an elephant,' which is patently untrue.

Such replies are not evidence against the cooperative principle. On the contrary, they simply show how strongly it works: people are so convinced that the other person in a conversation is being cooperative, that a superficial breakdown in a conversational maxim is treated as important and informative. For example, if someone said: 'What's for supper?' and the reply was the superficially irrelevant one: 'Billy fell downstairs,' the hearer is likely to assume that the information about Billy was somehow important, and will fill in the gaps with assumptions such as 'Since Billy was supposed to cook the supper, and he's fallen downstairs, I assume that there isn't any supper ready.' Similarly, if someone told an overt lie, such as 'Pamela's an elephant,' the listener would not just think, 'That's impossible,' they would cast around as to why the speaker had made this comment. In brief, listeners interpret what people say as conforming to the cooperative principle, even when this principle is overtly broken. They draw implications from the utterance which are not strictly there in the linguistic meaning.

Speech acts

When a person utters a sequence of words, the speaker is often trying to achieve some effect with those words, an effect which might in some cases have been accomplished by an alternative action. The words 'Get back!' might convey the same notion as a push.

(I state that:) *Violets are blue.*

This overall approach is known as **speech act** theory, and it is another method by which philosophers and linguists have tried to classify the ways in which humans use language, in this case by treating it as parallel to other actions which humans perform.

Proponents of speech act theory try, in the first place, to list the various possible speech acts which a speaker might attempt to perform – statements, requests, queries, commands, promises, placing of bets, and so on. The lists vary from writer to writer, though the overall core tends to be similar. At the heart of the list come statements, questions and commands:

(I state that:) *It's cold.*
(I ask you:) *What's the time?*
(I command you:) *Go away!*

These are examples of **direct speech acts**: the act is expressed overtly by the most obvious linguistic means.

But many speech acts are **indirect**, in that they possess the syntactic structure more usually associated with another act. For example, the following might all be intended as commands, yet only the first has the typical command structure:

Go to bed!
Isn't it past your bedtime?
You should have been in bed long ago.

The first is therefore a direct speech act, but the second two are indirect speech acts.

> Mother: *And how's my pretty little darling then?*
> Baby: *Ugh ... Ugh.*
> Mother: *O what a nice bit of wind that was! You must be feeling better!*
> Baby: *Goo, goo.*

This brief snatch of 'conversation' illustrates one important fact about human speech: people take it in turns to talk. Even if one of the participants cannot speak, the other one pretends that the non-talker has taken their turn. But we can go further than simply noting the phenomenon of turn-taking. We can, in addition, describe how a typical conversation might proceed. The speakers are taking part in a social ritual partially prescribed by convention. In a dialogue, utterances often occur in pairs:

> Question: *What's the time?*
> Answer: *Ten past three.*

> Greeting: *Hi, Jo.*
> Greeting: *Why hallo, Bill.*

> Offer: *Would you like a cup of coffee?*
> Acceptance: *Yes, please.*

> Apology: *I'm terribly sorry.*
> Minimization: *Please don't mention it.*

Paired utterances are not, of course, inevitable, and triple utterances are also frequent:

> Question: *What's the time?*
> Answer: *Ten past three.*
> Acknowledgement: *Thanks.*

Repairs

Conversations do not necessarily run smoothly. People cannot always explain things properly. Or they make a mistake.

Or the person they are talking to makes a mistake. These minor breakdowns, if noticed, have to be 'repaired'. So-called **repairs** can give additional insights into the way in which humans comprehend one another.

Repairs sometimes involve **self-repair**, when a speaker spontaneously notices a problem and solves it:

> *Could you hand me a spoon? A teaspoon, that is.*
> *Marion arrived on Saturday — sorry, I mean Sunday.*

Sometimes they involve **other-repair**, when someone is not quite sure about what has been said, or suspects that the other person has made a mistake.

> *I assume you mean a teaspoon.*
> *Did Marion really arrive on Saturday? Wasn't it Sunday?*

However, humans do not usually confront one another directly, a listener mildly queries the speaker, who then repairs the original utterance:

> Speaker A: *Alan's taken a course in deep-sea diving.*
> Speaker B: *Alan? Has he really?*
> Speaker A: *Sorry, I don't mean Alan, I mean Alec.*

As this example suggests, humans tend to be polite to one another, so politeness can radically affect the structure of conversations.

Politeness

> *Shut the door!*
> *I wonder if you'd mind shutting the door.*
> *There's quite a draught in here.*

If you wanted someone to shut the door, you could in theory use any of the sentences above. But in practice, the first, a direct command, would be uttered perhaps only to a young child. To anyone else, it would seem somewhat rude.

This avoidance of directness is partly culturally based: 'Why did that man look offended when I said, "Pass the salt"?' asked one puzzled visitor. She was even more bewildered when told that it would be better to say: 'I wonder if you could possibly pass the salt.' Why such a fuss, she queried, about a small quantity of salt? But in spite of cultural variation, the idea that it is politer to say things indirectly may be universal.

Humans everywhere tend to be polite in similar ways, based on two basic social requirements: 'No criticism' and 'No interference'. Humans want to be approved of, and they do not want to be imposed upon. Consequently, anyone with social know-how will minimize criticism of others and will avoid interfering with their liberty, at least overtly.

These requirements of 'No criticism' and 'No interference' have an effect on language. Any criticism or interference will be a social risk. Therefore speakers have to balance up the advantages and disadvantages of 'straight talking'. They must tot up the social distance between themselves and those they are talking to, the power relationship, the cultural norms, and make a decision.

But suppose someone had an urgent request, and felt obliged to impose on another person, what happens? There are various strategies which are used to soothe the situation. For example, anyone imposing is often pessimistic:

I don't suppose you could lend me a pound, could you?

Or they might try to minimize the imposition:

I won't keep you a minute, but ...

Or they might just apologize:

I'm terribly sorry to bother you, but ...

The various strategies occur worldwide, but they are not all necessarily found in every language. Each culture has its own preferred strategies.

10

language and society

This chapter is concerned with sociolinguistics, which analyzes variation within a language. It looks at differences between speech and writing, at variation in pronunciation between different social classes, and briefly discusses the linguistic study of social networks. It also outlines differences between men's and women's speech, and briefly mentions multilingual communities.

Sociolinguistics is often defined as the study of language and society. Whereas many linguists concentrate on discovering unity beneath the diversity of human languages, sociolinguists try to analyse the social factors which lead to this diversity. In brief, sociolinguists are interested in language differences, and especially in variation within a particular language.

The notion of a language

Perhaps the first question that a sociolinguist needs to ask is, 'What is a language?' Can the notion of 'a language' be defined geographically? Can it be equated with nationality? Or should a language be defined by the mutual intelligibility of its speakers?

The answer to all these questions appears to be 'no'. A geographical definition of a language would separate Australian, British and American English, which is obviously unsatisfactory. Nationality is a vague notion which has little to do with the language a person speaks. Numerous Russian Jews, for example, regard themselves as essentially Jewish, yet speak Russian. Mutual intelligibility is of little help, since a Glaswegian and a Cockney are likely to find it harder to understand one another than a Dutchman and a German who are considered to be speaking distinct languages.

Faced with this dilemma, sociolinguists prefer to start with the notion of a **speech community** rather than a 'language'. And they define a speech community as any group of people who consider that they speak the same language. Consequently, Dutch and German must be regarded as separate languages, since, in spite of their similarities, the Dutch consider that they speak Dutch and the Germans consider that they speak German. And all the Chinese dialects must be classified as one language, because, in spite of far-reaching differences, their speakers all consider that they speak Chinese.

Dialect and accent

Within a speech community, there is considerable language variation. The speech of its members varies according to many factors, including geographical location, age, occupation, socio-economic status, ethnic group and sex.

The most obvious type of variety in a speech community is the use of different **dialects**. A dialect is usually associated with a particular geographical area, such as the Geordie and Cockney dialects of English, which are spoken in Tyneside and London respectively. The term 'dialect' refers to far greater difference than mere pronunciation.

Unfortunately, in everyday usage, the term **dialect** is often confused with the word **accent**. An accent refers only to a difference in pronunciation. A Scotsman and a Londoner are likely to speak English with different accents. But if the underlying system and the vocabulary are the same, they will be speaking the same dialect.

From high to low

More interesting to sociolinguists is variation within a single geographical area. This is of two main types: variation within the speech of a single person, and variation between people. These two interact, and it is not always possible to separate them.

Every native speaker is normally in command of several different language styles, sometimes called **registers**, which are varied according to the topic under discussion, the formality of the occasion, and the medium used (speech, writing or sign).

Adapting language to suit the topic is a fairly straightforward matter. Many activities have a specialized vocabulary. If you are playing a ball game, you need to know that 'zero' is a *duck* in cricket, *love* in tennis, and *nil* in soccer. If you have a drink with friends in a pub, you need to know greetings such as: *Cheers! Here's to your good health!*

Other types of variation are less clear-cut. The same person might utter any of the following three sentences, depending on the circumstances:

I should be grateful if you would make less noise.
Please be quiet.
Shut up!

Here the utterances range from a **high** or formal style, down to a **low** or informal one – and the choice of a high or low style is partly a matter of politeness.

But politeness is just one component of a more general skill, the **appropriate** use of language. Knowing *what* to say *when* is sometimes known as **communicative competence**. Native speakers just 'know' it would be odd to say 'Kindly refrain from smoking' to a 10-year-old puffing at a stolen cigarette, or rude to say 'Put that fag out' to a duchess. Both utterances are equally inappropriate. Children and foreign learners have to acquire this skill over a longish period.

An inability to use appropriate language often makes a speaker sound very funny, so much so that the use of an inappropriate register is one source of humour in English, as in:

Scintillate, scintillate, globule lucific,
Fain would I fathom thy nature specific.

This seems amusing because of the use of a formal style to 'translate' a rhyme associated with an informal nursery setting:

Twinkle, twinkle, little star
How I wonder what you are.

Speech versus writing

Speech and writing differ in a number of ways.
They can be summed up in the following table:

Spoken	Written
More than one participant	Single writer
Inexplicit	Explicit
Repetitive	Non-repetitive
Fragments	Full sentences
Simple structure	Elaborate structure
Concrete, common vocabulary	Abstract, less common vocabulary

Figure 10.1.

Several of these features overlap with the formality–
informality scale, with speech containing informal features, and
written language formal ones. Consequently, formal speech has
quite a lot in common with informal writing.

Spoken language typically involves the characteristics in
the left-hand column of Figure 10.1, and written language those
in the right-hand column – though each can borrow from the
other. There is no hard and fast divide. A sermon is likely to have
more 'written' characteristics than a chat between friends in a
pub. One is not 'better' than the other; each is appropriate in
certain circumstances.

Charting phonological variation

Speakers vary not only their vocabulary and syntax, but
also the sound structure. Phonological variation, both between
speakers and within a single speaker, is important as a reflection
of various social factors. Speakers of a language alter their
phonology to suit a particular situation, often without realizing it.

At one time, it was thought that such variation was fairly
random, and that no precise statements could be made about it.
But an American sociolinguist, William Labov, showed that this
was not so. In a piece of work which has now become famous he
examined the pronunciation of words such as *car*, *park* in New
York. New Yorkers sometimes pronounce an [r] in these words,

and sometimes do not. Although Labov was unable to tell which words were likely to be pronounced with [r], and which without, he found that he could predict the percentage of [r] sounds which each socio-economic class and each age group would use in any given type of speech.

At first, one might assume Labov's results to be unique, in that they possibly reflected an American social situation that was unlikely to be paralleled elsewhere. But in England, a similar state of affairs has been found in the speech of people living in Norwich.

Social networks

Labov-type surveys rely on collecting data from a random sample of individuals. Their speech is analysed for various key characteristics, which are then correlated with their socio-economic background. The result, perhaps not surprisingly, suggests that human society is somewhat like a layer-cake, with different socio-economic layers stacked up on top of one another. In one respect, this is a useful insight into the way societies function. But, as with many surveys, the result is oversimplified. In practice, people do not normally live in such clear-cut layers: someone from the so-called working class might well have middle-class friends and neighbours.

In fact, human beings tend to cluster into **social networks**, groups of people who regularly interact with one another. A detailed study of the social networks within one particular speech community can provide a useful corrective to Labov-type studies, which tend to suggest humans are rigidly stratified. Network studies can provide a more realistic picture of the way people interact in real life.

The British linguists Jim and Lesley Milroy pioneered the linguistic study of social networks with a study of three communities in Belfast. Lesley was introduced into each group as 'a friend of a friend'. This ensured that she was accepted, and that people would talk relatively normally in front of her: when one youth tried to show off by talking in a somewhat affected

High-density network   Low-density network

Figure 10.2.

way, his friend punched him and shouted: 'Come on, you're not on television now, you know.'

Networks can be of high density, when the same people tend to work, play and live together. On the other hand, they can be of low density, when people only have a small amount of contact with any one network, in that they may live in one area, work in another, and travel elsewhere for their social life (Figure 10.2).

Language and sex

Possible sex differences in language usage have recently attracted a lot of attention.

First, we need to sort out whether women really do speak differently from men. People's impressions are not necessarily correct: it is often assumed, for example, that women talk more than men, whereas almost all research on the topic has demonstrated the opposite, that men talk more than women.

The most consistent difference found between men and women within the Western world is a tendency for women to speak in a way that is closer to the prestige standard. In colloquial terms, they speak 'better' than men. No one is quite sure why this is so, and several explanations have been proposed, which may all be partially right. For example, women may be pressurized by society to behave in a 'lady-like' manner, and 'speaking nicely' may be part of this. Or because they are the main child-rearers, they may subconsciously speak in a way which will enable their children to progress socially.

Furthermore, some characteristics attributed to women turn out to be far more widespread. For example, women have been claimed to use more **hedges**, tentative phrases such as *kind of*, *sort of*, in place of straight statements: 'Bill is kind of short,' instead of 'Bill is short.' They have also been accused of using question intonation in response to queries: 'About eight o'clock?' as a reply to: 'What time's dinner?' Yet this insecure style of conversation seems to be typical of 'powerless' people, those who are somewhat nervous and afraid of antagonizing others. Powerless people come from either sex.

But there is an alternative explanation: such speech may be **supportive**. A question intonation promotes the flow of conversation. A comment such as: 'It's cold today, isn't it?' encourages an easy-to-make response, such as: 'Yes, I even put my winter boots on.' 'Powerless' speech can therefore be viewed as friendly and cooperative, and powerful speech as insensitive and authoritarian.

Friendly speech may also reflect the setting. At a meeting, fairly formal speech is the norm. At home, or in the shops, informal conversation is more likely. Traditionally, men are more likely to be at business meetings, and women at home, though this is partly changing.

'Powerful' speakers typically control the topic, interrupt others, and demand explicit explanations. Occasionally, this may be justified if someone is chairing a meeting, or in some teaching situations.

Power talking may be used by either sex, though it is more typically male. Male speakers not only talk more, they also interrupt more, even though they may not perceive themselves as doing so.

Men also issue more direct orders. In a study of doctor–patient interaction in the USA, men used explicit commands in about one-third of the directives, as: 'Lie down', 'Take off your shoes and socks'. Women preferred to phrase commands as joint actions: 'Maybe we should just take the top of your dress off?', 'Maybe what we ought to do is stay with the dose you're on,' and so on.

Multilingual communities

'I speak Spanish to God, Italian to women, French to men, and German to my horse,' is a saying attributed to the Holy Roman Emperor Charles V. As this quotation suggests, in some cultures a changed social situation is marked by a change in the actual language spoken, a phenomenon known as **code-switching**. Sociolinguistically, this is not very different from stylistic variation within a single language. Sociolinguists have therefore become interested in studying code-switching in bilingual and multilingual communities.

A study of the ways in which these multiple languages are used is particularly important for **language planning**, a situation in which a government or education authority attempts to manipulate the linguistic situation in a particular direction. This is more likely to be successful if existing uses of a language are gradually extended, since the sudden imposition of a particular language by decree may well result in failure.

11

language
and mind

This chapter looks at psycholinguistics. It explains where psycholinguists find their evidence, and outlines how children acquire language, how adults comprehend speech, and how they produce it.

Psycholinguistics is often defined as the study of language and the mind. It explores what goes on in the human mind as an individual acquires, comprehends, produces and stores language.

Psycholinguistic evidence

The mind cannot be directly observed, so psycholinguists have to devise ways of finding out how it works. They get their evidence from two main sources: observation of spontaneous utterances, on the one hand, and psycholinguistic experiments, on the other.

Spontaneous utterances which deviate from the norm in some way are the most informative. We can learn considerably more from a child's mistake such as *foots* instead of 'feet', or someone who said *geranium* instead of 'hydrangea', than we can from a perfect flow of speech.

However, ordinary speech is somewhat messy, in that there are dozens of different factors which have to be taken into account when utterances are analysed. Psycholinguists therefore devise experiments in which the number of variable factors can be controlled, and the results can be accurately measured.

Ideally, major topics should be tackled both by observing spontaneous speech and by devising experiments. And when the results coincide, this is a sign that progress is being made.

Acquiring language

It used to be thought that animal behaviour could be divided into two types: that which was inborn and natural (for example, dogs naturally bark), and that which was learned and unnatural (dogs may be taught to beg). It turns out, however, that this division is by no means clear-cut and may be misleading. Many types of behaviour develop 'naturally' at a certain age, provided that the surrounding environment is adequate. Such behaviour is maturationally controlled, and sexual activity is a typical example. Arguments as to whether it is inborn or learnt are futile.

Both nature and nurture are important. Innate potentialities lay down the framework, and within this framework, there is wide variation depending on the environment. When individuals reach a crucial point in their maturation, they are biologically in a state of readiness for learning the behaviour. They would not learn it at this time without a biological trigger and, conversely, the biological trigger could not be activated if there was nobody around from whom they could learn the behaviour.

Human infants pay attention to language from birth. They produce recognizable words at around 12–15 months, and start putting words together at around 18 months. The urge for language to emerge at this time is very strong, and only extraordinary circumstances will suppress it – as in the case of Genie, a Californian teenager who from the age of 20 months had been confined to one small room, and had been physically punished by her father if she made any sounds. Naturally, she was without speech when she was found.

But all normal children, and some abnormal ones, will begin to speak if they hear language going on around them.

The content–process controversy

Most psycholinguists now agree that human beings are innately programmed to speak. But they cannot agree on exactly *what* is innate. In particular, they cannot decide to what extent (if any) language ability is separate from other cognitive abilities.

All researchers agree that there is extraordinary similarity in the speech development of English-speaking children. Children who could not possibly be acquainted go through similar stages in their development, and also make similar mistakes. The implications of this coincidence are hotly disputed. On the one hand, there are those who consider that this uniformity of speech development indicates that children innately *contain* a blueprint for language: this view represents a so-called **content** approach. Extreme supporters of this view suggest that children may have a universal framework imprinted on their brains.

On the other hand, there are those who support a **process** approach, and argue that children could not possibly contain specific language universals. Instead, they are innately geared to *processing* linguistic data, for which they utilize a puzzle-solving ability which is closely related to other cognitive skills.

The rule-governed nature of child language

In spite of the numerous controversies surrounding child language, psycholinguists are at least in agreement on one major point. Children are not simply imitating what they hear going on around them as if they were parrots. The learning processes involved are far more complex. Child language is never at any time a haphazard conglomeration of random words, or a sub-standard version of adult speech. Instead, every child at every stage possesses a grammar with rules of its own even though the system will be simpler than that of an adult. For example, when children first use negatives, they normally use a simple rule: 'Put *no* or *not* in front of the sentence.' This results in consistent negative sentences which the child could not possibly have heard from an adult:

> *No play that.*
> *No Fraser drink all tea.*

A rather more obvious example of the rule-governed nature of child language are forms such as *mans*, *foots*, *gooses*, which children produce frequently. Such plurals occur even when a child understands and responds correctly to the adult forms *men*, *feet*, *geese*. This is clear proof that children's own rules of grammar are more important to them than mere imitation.

Children do not, however, formulate a new rule overnight, and suddenly replace the old one with a new one. Instead, there is considerable fluctuation between the old and the new. The new construction appears at first in a limited number of places. A child might first use the word *what* in a phrase with a single verb:

What mummy doing?
What daddy doing?
What Billy doing?

then only gradually extend it to other verbs, as in:

What kitty eating?
What mummy sewing?

Different children use different strategies for acquiring speech. For example, some seem to concentrate on the overall rhythm, and slot in words with the same general sound pattern, whereas others prefer to deal with more abstract slots. Of particular interest is work which looks at how children cope with different languages. This enables researchers to see if children have any universal expectations about how language behaves, or whether they wait and see what their own particular language offers.

Learning the meaning of words

Children have to learn not only the syntax and sounds of their language, but also the meaning of words. This turns out to be more complicated than some people suppose. For a start, it probably takes some time for children to discover that words can refer to separate things. At first, they probably think that a word such as *milk* refers to a whole generalized ritual, something uttered as a mug is placed in front of them. Later, they discover that words have meanings which can be applied to individual objects and actions.

At first, children may use a word only in a particular context. One child agreed that *snow* was white, but refused to accept that a piece of paper was also white. This tendency to **undergeneralize** often passes unnoticed. But it is probably commoner than **overgeneralization**, which attracts much more attention.

Recognizing words

Understanding speech is not the simple matter it appears to be at first sight. Hearers, it is often supposed, behave like secretaries taking down a mental dictation. They mentally record the message, then read it back to themselves.

This assumption turns out to be quite wrong. For a start, it is physically impossible to recognize each separate sound, speech is just too fast. Understanding language is an *active*, not a passive process. Hearers jump to conclusions on the basis of partial information. This has been demonstrated in various experiments. For example, listeners were asked to interpret the following sentences, in which the first sound of the final word was indistinct.

Paint the fence and the ?ate.
Check the calendar and the ?ate.
Here's the fishing gear and the ?ate.

The subjects claimed to hear *gate* in the first sentence, *date* in the second, and *bait* in the third.

Since recognizing words involves quite a lot of guesswork, how do speakers make the guesses? Suppose someone had heard 'She saw a do–'. Would the hearer check through the possible candidates one after the other, *dog*, *doll*, *dot*, *dock*, and so on? Or would all the possibilities be considered subconsciously at the same time?

The human mind, it appears, prefers the second method, that of parallel processing, so much so that even unlikely possibilities are probably considered subconsciously. The mind is an enormously powerful network in which any word which at all resembles the one heard is automatically activated, and that each of these triggers its own neighbours, so that activation gradually spreads like ripples on a pond. Words that seem particularly appropriate get more and more excited, and those which are irrelevant gradually fade away. Eventually, one candidate wins out over the others.

Understanding syntax

We now know quite a lot about word recognition. But it is still unclear how separate words are woven together into the overall pattern.

To some extent, the process is similar to word recognition, in that people look for outline clues, and then actively reconstruct the probable message from them. They jump to conclusions on the basis of outline clues by imposing what they expect to hear onto the stream of sounds. For example, consider the sentence:

The boy kicked the ball threw it back.

Most people who hear this sentence feel that there is something wrong with it, that there is a word left out somewhere, and that it would preferably be:

*The boy **who** kicked the ball threw it back.*
The boy kicked the ball, then threw it back.

However, they realize that it is in fact perfectly well formed when shown a similar sentence:

The boy thrown the ball kicked it back. (The boy to whom the ball was thrown kicked it back.)

The problem arose because when interpreting sentences, people tend to impose a subject–verb–object sequence on them.

Speech production

Speech production involves at least two types of process. On the one hand, words have to be selected. On the other, they have to be integrated into the syntax.

Slips of the tongue – cases in which the speaker accidentally says something such as *par cark* instead of 'car park' – provide useful clues to these processes, and so do pauses: they can tell us where a speaker stops to think – though it is difficult to separate out pauses caused by searching for lexical items, and pauses due to syntactic planning.

There are two main kinds of slip: on the one hand, there are **selection errors**, cases in which a speaker has picked out the wrong item, as in:

Please hand me the tin-opener (nut-crackers).
Your seat's in the third component (compartment).

On the other hand, there are **assemblage errors**, cases in which a correct choice has been made, but the utterance has been wrongly assembled:

Dinner is being served at wine (Wine is being served at dinner).
A poppy of my caper (A copy of my paper).

Selection errors usually involve lexical items, so they can tell us which words are closely associated in the mind. For example, people tend to say *knives* for 'forks', *oranges* for 'lemons', *left* for 'right', suggesting that words on the same general level of detail are tightly linked, especially if they are thought of as a pair. Similar-sounding words which get confused tend to have similar beginnings and endings, and a similar rhythm, as in *antidote* for 'anecdote', *confusion* for 'conclusion'.

Whereas selection errors tell us how individual words are stored and selected, assemblage errors indicate how whole sequences are organized ready for production. Mistakes nearly always take place within a single 'tone group' – a short stretch of speech spoken with a single intonation contour. This suggests that the tone group is the unit of planning. And within the tone group, items with similar stress are often transposed, as in:

A gas of tank (A tank of gas).

Furthermore, when sounds are switched, initial sounds change place with other initials, and final with final, and so on, as in:

Reap of hubbish (Heap of rubbish).
Hass or grash (Hash or grass).

All this suggests that speech is organized in accordance with a rhythmic principle – that a tone group is divided into smaller units (usually called feet), which are based (in English) on stress. Feet are divided into syllables, which are in turn possibly controlled by a biological 'beat' which regulates the speed of utterance.

12

language and style

This chapter looks at literary language, and discusses where it overlaps with, and where it differs from 'ordinary' language. It also briefly discusses the language of advertising and newspaper language.

'Philosophy will clip an angel's wings,' according to the nineteenth-century poet, John Keats. Likewise, many have been unwilling to dissect literature, fearing analysis would destroy its magic.

But literary language is not a bizarre confection of angel-dust. Instead, it overlaps strongly with various other types of language, including everyday language. At one time, literature was thought to break linguistic 'rules'. Nowadays, the belief that 'real' rules can be firmly specified and divided from 'broken' rules has faded: language is flexible and fuzzy-edged.

In addition, the label 'literature' has been reassessed. Literature is 'highly valued writing', and non-literature is 'lowly valued writing' – just as a flower is a desired plant, and a weed an unwanted one. The judgement varies, depending on the judge: values alter from generation to generation. What is prized in one century may be condemned in the next. And at all times, 'good' literature merges into 'bad', with no firm dividing-line.

Style and stylistics

The linguistic analysis of literary language is known as **stylistics**.

Literary language often deviates from everyday language, even though it is in no way deviant. Typically, certain features have been highlighted, or **foregrounded**, often by making them strange. **Foregrounding** has two intertwined meanings. On the one hand, it involves bringing forward literary usages against the background of expectations about ordinary usage. On the other hand, certain features are made prominent or foregrounded within a text. As the term foregrounding suggests, literary language is intentionally compared with the visual arts, where an artist is likely to emphasize some aspects of a painting over others.

A poem about the wind is likely to differ from, say, a chat about the weather. But poetry cannot be too peculiar, or readers and listeners would simply 'turn off'. Only a small and predictable proportion of language can be varied.

The same bright, patient stars

'And still they were the same bright, patient stars,' said Keats in his poem *'Hyperion'*. And in literary language the phonology, morphology and (mostly) the syntax are the same bright, patient stars. They may sometimes deviate from the norm, but do so relatively little.

Take phonology. 'Be wery careful o' vidders [widows] all your life,' says Mr Weller in Charles Dickens' *Pickwick Papers*, his Cockney accent signalled primarily by the switch of *v* and *w*. Non-standard accents are usually represented, as here, via only occasional changes to the normal spelling.

Syntax may deviate more than morphology, though any deviation is likely to be minor, as:

> **And like a dying lady, lean and pale,**
> **Who totters forth, wrapped in a gauzy veil,**
>
> Percy Bysshe Shelley

> **I see a lily on thy brow,**
> **With anguish moist and fever dew;**
>
> John Keats

Ways with words

Words are the wool out of which literature is knitted. Yet these are mainly existing ones, used in novel ways: brand new words are relatively rare in serious writing.

A bunch of oldish words are sometimes thought of as poetic, such as *quoth, fain, behold*, as also are some conventional abbreviations: *o'er, 'twas, ne'er*. Yet these have always been sparsely used, and most are now unusual even in literature.

Writers are like knitters trying to invent new patterns. They avoid obvious sequences such as *black despair, green fingers* or *purple patch*, and devise new, original combinations. 'And then the lover/Sighing like a furnace ...', said Shakespeare.

Twisting words

The name *trope* comes originally from the Greek word for twisting or turning. **Simile** is possibly the most straightforward. It involves an explicit comparison of two unlike things, as in 'Fame is like a river'.

Metaphor is perhaps the best known trope, once defined by the Greek philosopher Aristotle as 'the application to one thing of a name belonging to another'. For example, 'Fame is a food' ('Fame is a food that dead men eat,' once said by the poet Austin Dobson), when fame is clearly *not* something which can be literally devoured.

Metaphor is sometimes assumed to be fundamentally poetic in nature. And poetry does indeed teem with metaphor; but so does everyday speech. Metaphor is an inevitable part of day-to-day language, as in:

Pauline's a gold-digger.
Felix tried to get his ideas across.
Marigold shot down his arguments.

And so on, and so on. It is impossible to do without it, especially in areas where drama is low, such as finance:

The dollar tumbled to a new low.
Will our bubble economy go pop?

Yet many everyday metaphors are stale: clichés such as *black mood*, *white lie* are sometimes even labelled 'dead metaphors'. Poetic metaphors are fresh. And more often than in ordinary conversation, they conjure up a whole novel scene, as in Shakespeare's famous line:

Sleep, which knits up the ravelled sleeve of care.

Here *sleep* does not relate to only one word; instead a whole knitting scenario is envisaged.

Quality rather than quantity, then, is what distinguishes poetic metaphors from everyday ones.

> *The moan of doves in immemorial elms,*
> *And murmuring of innumerable bees.*
>
> **Lord Alfred Tennyson**

These lines of Tennyson are often quoted as an instance of 'poetic' writing. They attempt to reproduce the sound of doves cooing and bees humming, technically, **onomatopoeia**. This drowsy hum effect has been created above all by **repetition**, in this case mainly of the sounds *m* and *r*.

Repetition is a glue which helps a work of literature to hang together as a whole, or **cohere**. Of course, real-life conversation is enormously repetitious, as: 'Football, football, everybody keeps talking about football.' The planned and patterned nature of literary repetition is what distinguishes it from everyday repeats.

Rhyme and metre are types of repetition strongly associated with poetry. In rhyme, the ends of words are repeated, as in:

> *That orbèd maiden with white fire laden,*
> *Whom mortals call the Moon,*
> *Glides glimmering o'er my fleece-like floor,*
> *By the midnight breezes strewn.*
>
> **Percy Bysshe Shelley**

Poetic metre may at first sight seem artificial, with recurring types of *foot* (unit of rhythm). Yet poetry does not use bizarre, invented beats. Instead, it is ultimately based on spoken language. Large chunks of it are written in the *dum-di dum-di* 'Monday, Tuesday ...', 'bread 'n' butter' pattern widely found in everyday speech, as in:

> *Tyger! Tyger! burning bright*
> *In the forests of the night ...*
>
> **William Blake**

Saying it again, but subtly

> **By the shores of Gitche Gumee**
> **By the shining Big-Sea-Water,**
> **Stood the wigwam of Nokomis,**
> **Daughter of the Moon, Nokomis ...**
>
> Henry W. Longfellow

These lines from 'Hiawatha' contain obvious repetition. Yet much of literature hangs together via less obvious repetitious devices. 'Hiawatha' continues:

> **Dark behind it rose the forest,**
> **Rose the black and gloomy pine-trees,**
> **Rose the firs with cones upon them ...**

Firs and pines are both types of tree, and a collection of trees makes up a forest. The poet assumes that the readers know all this.

Yet repetition, or near-repetition, plays only a partial role. Above all, successful literary works have an underlying structure – and so do many other forms of language.

Searching for the skeleton: poems, news

Words are like the flesh on an underlying skeleton. The bones vary in their rigidity. Some verse is tightly formed: sonnets have a fourteen-line structure, and limericks a five-line one.

Other written forms have a less obvious structure. Take newspaper reports. It is fashionable to moan about 'journalese'. Yet this is unwarranted. The vocabulary and style are straightforward.

What *is* complex is the structure underlying the news stories. New information is placed first within a *what-where-(when)-who-how-(why)* summary, a so-called **hard news**

formula whose purpose is to orient the reader fast as to *what* happened, *where* it happened, *who* was involved, *how* it occurred, and *why* it happened – though *when* is often missing, because news is assumed to be new and recent, and *why* is not always known. For example:

> *At least 26 people were killed and more than 200 injured when a huge car bomb ripped through the centre of Omagh, County Tyrone, yesterday afternoon.*

A huge amount of important information is tightly packed into that first sentence, which provides a concise account of the whole event – a summary that only skilled journalists can easily write, and the headline is commonly written from that summary.

After the summary, the story consists of a sequence of events, though not necessarily in order of occurrence: the most recent come first. A high level of skill is required to present this information clearly, and in an interesting fashion. Eventually comes a final sentence outlining the current 'state of play' – though this must never contain crucial information, because it is likely to be cut if space is short.

The language of advertising

> *Musk. The missing link between animal and man. Earthy, Primitive. Fiercely masculine.* (Cosmetic advertisement)

Advertising copywriters, like journalists, have to present their message briefly, and in an eye-catching way.

If verbs are used in the main message of an advertisement, they are often imperatives:

> *Drinka pinta milka day.*
> *Go to work on an egg.*

If they are not imperatives, they are almost always in the present tense, and negatives are rare:

Persil washes whiter.
Oxo gives a meal man appeal.
You can take a White Horse anywhere.

There's likely to be a pun somewhere: 'The colour of the sun – puts the rest in the shade.' It's easy to think up other examples of plays on words in well-known ads:

Better in jams than strawberries. (Car advertisement)
Players please. (Cigarette advertisement)

These strategies are not only used to make people buy particular shampoos or perfumes. They are also utilized by politicians, as in the slogans of political parties:

Let's go with Labour. (Labour party slogan)
Labour isn't working. (Conservative party slogan)

But not all 'advertising' is so straightforward. Less obvious, and so more dangerous, are some of the other techniques used by politicians, such as the use of metaphor. Subtle and skilful use of metaphor can influence people's thoughts in a way in which they may be unaware. The *arms race* is a classic example. Politicians sometimes pretend that their nation is in an athletic contest with other nations, even though this may be entirely in their imagination.

These days, nuclear weapons attract a high number of metaphors. These hideously dangerous devices tend to be referred to by politicians as 'nuclear shields' or 'nuclear deterrents', or a 'nuclear umbrella'. This leads people to believe that they are genuinely necessary (we all need umbrellas), purely defensive (shields), and even useful in discouraging others from warfare (deterrents). These beliefs may, or may not, be true. But the language used in discussing nuclear armaments ensures that the average person does not look beyond the reassuring language, and therefore fails to perceive the potential dangers involved.